2/13
Amazon

ARCADIA PUBLIC LIBRARY
ARCADIA, WI 54612

D0324359

PRAYERS
and
REFLECTIONS
FOR
NEWLYWEDS

Aaron A.
Del Monte

242.6
DEL

Liguori
LIGUORI, MISSOURI

Imprimi Potest:
Harry Grile, CSsR, Provincial
Denver Province, The Redemptorists

Published by Liguori Publications
Liguori, Missouri 63057

To order, call 800-325-9521, or visit liguori.org.

Copyright © 2012 Aaron A. Del Monte

All rights reserved. No part of this publication may be reproduced, stored in a retrieval system, or transmitted in any form or by any means—electronic, mechanical, photocopy, recording, or any other—except for brief quotations in printed reviews, without the prior written permission of Liguori Publications.

Library of Congress Cataloging-in-Publication Data
Del Monte, Aaron A.
  Prayers and reflections for newlyweds / Aaron A. Del Monte.—1st ed.
      p. cm.
  ISBN 978-0-7648-2085-4
  1. Newlyweds—Prayers and devotions. 2. Married people—Prayers and devotions. I. Title.
  BV4596.M3D44 2011
  242'.644—dc23
                              2011047750

Scripture quotations are from *New Revised Standard Version Bible*, copyright © 1989 National Council of the Churches of Christ in the United States of America. Used by permission. All rights reserved.

Liguori Publications, a nonprofit corporation, is an apostolate of the Redemptorists. To learn more about the Redemptorists, visit Redemptorists.com.

Printed in the United States of America

15 14 13 12 / 5 4 3 2 1

First Edition

CONTENTS

This book is dedicated to...

My wife, Sherry,
The love of my life.

My children, A.J., Angelina, and Analisa,
the greatest gifts I have ever received.

My parents, John and Mary Del Monte,
inspiring examples of lifelong love.

All married couples who, through their love,
grow closer to each other, grow closer to God,
and make our world a better place.

INTRODUCTION

Congratulations! By getting married, you are continuing one of the greatest journeys of your lifetime, one of relationship and love. You have both met "the one," someone you love unconditionally and someone with whom you feel complete. Sometimes it can seem like a miracle that you have both found each other. But you have—and now you have the rest of your lives to grow in your love and dreams together.

This book contains twelve chapters that tell the story of a married couple, from meeting and falling in love to getting married, facing challenges, and dreaming of a future together. The book can be read from start to finish, or you may choose to read the chapters in whatever order is most inspiring for you or your spouse.

Many newlyweds would like to pray more often but are unsure of exactly how to do so. My hope is that this book will offer some simple yet meaningful guidance for prayer and reflection.

Every chapter contains several poems and prayers, including Scripture verses with reflective text to help you understand and think about each passage. The chapters also contain a feature called *Looking Back, Looking Ahead,* which includes questions to help you reflect on the past and imagine the future of your marriage. Additional personal reflection prompts are included in a *Sharing Together* section for couples to talk about the chapter content, as well as a *Growing Together* section with activities that couples can do together to explore and nurture their relationship.

It is my sincere hope that this book will offer support for your relationship as you seek to grow closer to God and one another.

May God bless you with a lifetime of love,
happiness, and fulfillment together.

Chapter One

FALLING IN LOVE

Three things are too wonderful for me;
four I do not understand:
the way of an eagle in the sky,
the way of a snake on a rock,
the way of a ship on the high seas,
and the way of a man with a girl.

PROVERBS 30:18-19

Falling in love
is one of life's
wonderful mysteries.

*O*ur lives are surrounded by the sights and sounds of falling in love. As children, we heard stories about princes and princesses living happily ever after. As we grew older, we learned about the wonders of love from music, movies, and television. Today, shelves of romance novels line bookstores and supermarket displays.

Even the anticipation of falling in love can be a powerful experience. I remember lying in bed when I was young and wondering who I might fall in love with. What was her name, where did she live, and what she was doing right now?

What are your earliest memories of falling in love? Do you remember butterflies in your stomach from a childhood crush? My father first kissed a girl in kindergarten! Decades later, hours from our childhood home, our family miraculously ran into her. My father didn't recognize her at first, but then she asked, "Don't you recognize your first girlfriend?" My father, always poised, was speechless and red in the face, like a young schoolboy. Now that's powerful!

Falling in love involves attraction of all kinds. You may have many things in common or be completely different, but the attraction is there, pulling you closer and closer together. The more we learn about the other, the more we want to know. It's amazing!

Probably the only thing more amazing than falling in love is the fact that someone might actually fall in love with us. "How did I get so lucky?" you might recall thinking to yourself. When we experience someone who really loves us and wants to get to know us, we get excited, not only about each other, but about life.

Yes, "falling in love" is the first step toward any marriage, but it doesn't need to become a distant memory. The magic, mystery, and joy of falling in love never has to grow old and can be nurtured along the way. You and your partner are on a lifelong journey together. It is a journey of falling in love.

I had heard about love many times
But never felt its touch.
I never understood its depth or power,

And then you were there.

Within my busy life,
Emptiness filled its core.
Lots of activity, without purpose.

And then you were there.

Among the many, I still felt lonely.
There was no one I could open up to,
Nobody with whom I could
share my story, my life.

And then you were there.

I thank God I have you in my life.

I had heard about love many times
But never felt its touch.
I never understood its depth or power,

And then you were there.

God, we have fallen in love.

*As we continue to be drawn
to each other,
help us know that our love
is only a fraction of the love
you have for us.*

*Thank you for all
that has led us to this moment.*

*Help us to remember and cherish our past.
Help us to approach each day.*

*Help us to continue to fall in love
as we grow closer to each other
and closer to you each day.*

Amen.

My beloved thrust his hand into the opening,
and my inmost being yearned for him.

SONG OF SONGS 5:4

Love challenges us to make ourselves
vulnerable to each other.

Many waters cannot quench love,
  neither can floods drown it.
If one offered for love
  all the wealth of one's house,
  it would be utterly scorned.

SONG OF SONGS 8:7

No experience is more powerful
than finding true and lasting love.

Looking Back

Close your eyes and think about
when you first met.

Remember your first thoughts,
    your first conversation,
    your first date,
    your first decision
    to live a life together.
What did you hope for most when you first met?

Looking Ahead

Now think about the love you hold.
Think of future conversations,
shared fun, laughter, pain, and renewed love.

What do you hope for most?

Whisper one word
that captures your future dreams.

Love changes everything.

I know a young man who struggled with confidence,
despite being friendly, outgoing and multitalented.

Then he met a girl.

He was magically transformed!

Never one to dress to impress,
he is now sporting a new haircut,
wearing more stylish clothes,
and has a newfound air of confidence.
He even seems more expressive
and compassionate.

My wife and I ran into him and his date
at a local restaurant one night.

As we talked, I saw a sparkle in his eye,
and a look of pride and happiness on his face.
"He is falling in love," I thought.

Yes, love changes everything.

God, bless our love.

Bless the feelings we share
and transform them into
loving words and actions.

Bless the mystery of our relationship.

Give us the strength and wisdom
to be our best selves
as our love continues to grow.

Through the miracle of our love,
help us to appreciate every day together
as we continue to fall in love,
forever and forever.

Amen.

So how did you fall in love? What are your earliest memories of being together? When I met my wife, Sherry, we found out that we attended the same church. It's hard to believe, but our first date was at church!

Can you remember not just what you did but how you felt when you first started falling in love? Marriage is a lifetime of falling in love. Each day, every day, in new ways.

Sharing Together

✦ *What was your life like before you fell in love?*
  How is it better now?

✦ *What parts of your love relationship*
  do you never want to change?

✦ *What has falling in love taught you about yourself?*

Growing Together

✦ *Buy an inexpensive gift for each other that represents*
  something you admire or appreciate about the other
  person. Exchange gifts and share the meaning. You'll
  learn about each other and have a wonderful memento
  of your love!

✦ *Plan, cook, and share a meal together. Include foods*
  that bring back favorite memories of your relationship.
  Talk about your memories while you eat together.

Chapter Two

I FOUND
"THE ONE"

For where your treasure is,
there your heart will be also.

MATTHEW 6:21

Someone you love
can become the center
of your happiness.

*D*o you remember when you knew you had found "the one?" Is it a crystal-clear memory? Or a "knowing" that happened over time? My moment of certainty came when my wife, Sherry, and I had been dating about two years. Ironically, it is also a moment when our relationship almost ended.

We had talked about a life together, but we knew there were also obstacles to our future. The biggest obstacle for me was that Sherry was a smoker.

Sherry's smoking hadn't caused problems for us, but I knew it could take years from her life and bring possible birth defects and secondhand smoke to the children we both hoped to share.

Sherry wanted to quit—some day—and she knew it was real deal-breaker for me, for "us." Eventually she made a commitment to quit smoking.

I thought Sherry was doing fairly well until I stopped by one evening after work. Sherry answered the door with tears streaming down her face. I anxiously asked what was wrong and she led me to her bedroom. She was packing, and luggage covered the bed and much of the floor. She sat on her bed and began to cry uncontrollably. "What is going on?" I asked again.

"I can't do it, Aaron!" she cried. "I can't quit!" Between sobs, she told me I deserved to be married to a nonsmoker. She had smoked a cigarette and now she doubted she could ever quit. She had decided to go back to her family in Indiana and then asked me to drive her to the airport.

At that moment, I knew that Sherry was "the one" for me.

She felt like a failure, but I saw only the respect she had for my values, her honesty, and the fact that she had not hidden the truth, despite smoking only one cigarette. In that moment, I knew she was the person with whom I wanted to spend the rest of my life.

Our story has a happy ending. I told her I would stand by her as she tried to quit smoking. She decided not to move back home. I proposed a couple of months later, and our journey to marriage officially began.

Quitting proved more challenging than we ever imagined, and Sherry was still a smoker on our wedding day. But about a year later, she ended her habit once and for all.

I knew I had found "the one" amid sobs, suitcases, and a real commitment to one another. What's your story?

....

We may have never met
    if we had lived in different cities.

We may have never met
    if we had attended different schools.

We may have never met
    if we had worked in different places.

We may have never met
    if we had attended different churches.

We may have never met
    if we had different interests.

We may have never met
    if we did not have the courage
    to talk to each other
on that particular day.

When we look at the odds
    of meeting each other,
    chances are that it
    never should have happened.

It happened.

God, you brought us together
so that we could find lasting love
and happiness here on earth.

As we move forward
on our journey of love,
help us to always appreciate
and cherish your miracle
of finding one another.

Be with us as we seek
and share
our love together.

Always.
Amen.

I slept, but my heart was awake.
Listen! my beloved is knocking.
"Open to me, my sister, my love,
my dove, my perfect one!"

SONG OF SONGS 5:2

Love means sharing all the parts of who you are.

My beloved speaks and says to me:
"Arise, my love, my fair one,
and come away;
for now the winter is past,
the rain is over and gone.

SONG OF SONGS 2:10–11

*Love means believing in someone,
and looking to the future with hope.*

Looking Back

Think back to when you first met.
The moments that led to

> A deepening,
> A discovery,
> A decision to be together.

What was your greatest blessing?

Looking Ahead

Think toward your future as a couple
and the qualities you each bring
to your relationship.

Love supporting love,
Strength supporting strength.

> Growing together as
> you find lasting happiness.

What do you hope is your greatest blessing?

During college, my best friend and I
would go on weekend backpacking trips.

We often said that the test of true love
was whether "the one" would enjoy
backpacking as much as we did.

We thought
we would know
we had found our dream—
a "low-maintenance" woman.

Well, we both ended up marrying women
*who will **never** go backpacking,*

And we realized
some things
are more important
than "low maintenance."

God, bless our relationship.

Bless the qualities
you have given each of us.

Draw us to you
and to one another.

Bless the obstacles
that come our way
and strengthen our love.

Bless our bond
as we commit ourselves
more fully to you
and to one another
each day, every day.

Now and always,

Amen.

Today may appear to be an ordinary day.
But before the day ends, it will be extraordinary.
Today I will ask you to marry me.

I carefully chose your engagement ring.
Your family has given me their blessing,
and they know today is the day.

I have rehearsed this proposal
 a hundred times.

I know what I will say,
I know what I will ask.

The only thing I don't know
is what your answer will be.

A question that will change our lives
in a matter of seconds

Will you marry me?

What's your moment? When did you first realize you had found someone with whom you wanted to spend the rest of your life? Maybe you have a collection of moments, a special milestone, or a crisis where you knew you had found "the one."

Your moment gives you important clues about what will bring you genuine happiness in your years together. What drew you?

Sharing Together

✦ *Describe how you realized you wanted to spend the rest of your life with your spouse.*

✦ *What does your moment tell you about what you value in your relationship?*

✦ *How did you come to believe that God was calling you to spend your lives together in marriage?*

Growing Together

✦ *Write down the ten qualities you appreciate about the other person. Compare your lists.*

> *What surprised you?*
> *What warmed your heart?*

✦ *Ask someone to videotape you and your partner as you answer these questions:*

> *How did you meet each other?*
>
> *What do you find most attractive about each other?*
>
> *How did you know you were meant to spend the rest of your life together?*

Watch the video occasionally to remind you about the foundations of your relationship. It can also be a lot of fun for your children to watch some day!

Chapter Three

WE'RE ENGAGED!

O my dove, in the clefts of the rock,
in the covert of the cliff,
let me *see* your face,
let me hear your voice;
for your voice is *sweet*,
and your face is lovely.

SONG OF SONGS 2:14

Engagement is an
invitation to explore your
relationship more fully.

"Will you marry me?" These are some of the most profound words we will ever say or hear. They are an invitation to grow together in love for an entire lifetime!

A proposal reveals a lot about a relationship. It might be simple or elaborate, intimate or public, comical or profound. My proposal to Sherry was a simple one, surrounded by family.

One evening, after dinner at her grandmother's house, I handed Sherry's brother a video camera and asked him to start filming me. Then with Sherry's mother and grandmother looking on, I talked about how happy I was and what a great girlfriend I had in Sherry.

Sherry knew that I could be sentimental, so she didn't really think anything was out of the ordinary. But I will never forget the look of surprise and joy when I dropped to one knee, presented her with a ring, and asked her to marry me. And she said, "Yes!"

Sherry and I decided to be engaged for two years. We both wanted a large wedding, but our families lived 2,000 miles apart, so we knew our wedding would take quite a bit of planning. We also wanted to just enjoy being engaged.

For the next two years, we spent more time together than we ever had before. We talked a lot about our relationship, got to know each other's families more, took extended trips together, and went on a retreat at our church to learn more about ourselves as a couple.

Two years later, we knew our decision to get married was right for us. We were so excited! We found that engagement isn't just about wedding planning: It's about taking the time to find out if we could be happy together for a lifetime.

Be sure and give yourselves the time you need to explore your relationship beyond all the outside preparations for your wedding day. Engagement can be a wonderful time to find out what it means to be committed to each other from the inside out.

We are engaged!
And so much in love!

Our love is so strong,
*   at this moment*
*   complete happiness means*
*   a life together.*

God, be with us as we make this engagement
a time of growth and exploration.

Watch over us
*   as we discover what makes our love strong*
*   and what we can do to make our love flourish.*

Help us to be humble enough to listen to others,
*   to gather the wisdom of their experience,*
*   and to ponder their advice.*

Most of all,
help us keep you at the center of our engagement
in preparation for our life together.

The sentinels found me,
    as they went about in the city.
    "Have you seen him whom my soul loves?"

Scarcely had I passed them,
    when I found him whom my soul loves.
    I held him, and would not let him go.

SONG OF SONGS 3:3–4

If you have the opportunity to spend the rest of your life with "the one," don't waste the opportunity! Focus entirely on exploring the possibilities.

Keep your heart with all vigilance,
    for from it flow the springs of life.

PROVERBS 4:23

Take love seriously, for through it we find happiness.

Looking Back

Once upon a time,
you looked at each other and said, "Hello"
for the first time.

Now you look at each other,
And you have chosen to spend a life together.

When did you change from acquaintances to "something
more?"
When did you know that you wanted to be a married couple?

Looking Ahead

You are preparing for marriage!

Imagine your wedding day.
Not the dress, rings, music, or guests,
but simply the two of you.

What will you feel when you
gaze into each other's eyes that day?

> What thoughts cross your mind?
> What are you most excited about?

A close friend invited my wife and me to dinner.
He prepared an elegant meal, sat down with us,
and told us he had something important to say.

"I'm ready to get married."

"Did you meet someone?" we asked.
"No," he said. "It's just time."
We told him he was working backward.

But he didn't hear us.
The next woman he dated soon became his fiancée.
The engagement was filled with jealousy and conflict.

Friends and family urged him to reconsider.
Sadly, but predictably, the marriage ended badly.
My friend struggled through a slow, difficult recovery.

Then he called again.
He's engaged!
He's a little older, a little wiser.

This time, engagement will mean shared discovery.
He has truly found "the one."

Our engagement is so finite.
It began when a ring was given
and will end when rings are exchanged.

Bless this special time together
as our relationship continues to grow.

Bless our thoughts
as we envision and plan for the future.

Bless our conversations
as we care for and encourage one another.

Bless our love
as we prepare for a life together.

After Sherry put on her engagement ring and we celebrated with family members, we decided to go for a short drive for some quiet time alone. I vividly remember driving through town, hand-in-hand, looking at the diamond on her finger. Even though I had planned this proposal for weeks, I think it was only in that car ride that it all hit me. We're engaged! We're going to get married!

In that moment, everything felt different. I was in love with a great woman, and I really felt as if we were a team, ready to take on whatever life had in store.

Sharing Together

✦ *How did you feel after you were engaged?*

✦ *What makes you a great couple?*

✦ *What are some challenges you think you might face as a married couple? What might make things a little easier?*

Growing Together

✦ *Identify two to four couples you see as having strong, stable, and happy marriages. Talk with them about their marriage.*

✦ *Set aside some "retreat" time together. Talk about what you would share with another couple about what makes a great marriage.*

Chapter Four

THE WEDDING

I come to my garden, my *sister*, my bride;
I gather my myrrh with my *spice*,
I eat my honeycomb with my honey,
I drink my wine with my milk.
Eat, friends, drink,
and be drunk with love.

SONG OF SONGS 5:1

A wedding
is a celebration of love,
the beginning of a
lifelong commitment to
one another.

*Y*our wedding day is one of the most significant days in the life of your relationship. It is the day when you become a family and when you promise to grow together in love for your entire lives. Your wedding day gives you anniversaries to celebrate and an opportunity to reaffirm your love. What a powerful day! Events, emotions, and memories. A day that celebrates who you are and the beginning of who you will become.

Our wedding day was a festive, heartfelt celebration. We realized we wanted to be surrounded by family and friends, we wanted everyone to have fun, and we wanted everyone to feel welcome.

I remember looking at the guests at the wedding and the reception thinking to myself, "This is probably the greatest number of people who know us and care about us that we will ever see together in one place."

My favorite mementos from our wedding day are two letters that we were asked to write to each other about our getting married. We were surprised when the minister read parts of our letters aloud during the wedding ceremony. The words he read brought tears to everyone's eyes, and I understood our love even more clearly.

Expressing our love to one another and valuing the people who love us and support us has remained a constant since our wedding day. What began as one day of celebration has continued to sustain our lives together.

God, we are thankful
for each other
and our marriage.

Give us the wisdom
to appreciate and honor
our special commitment.

Help us remember
the love and excitement
of our wedding day
as we live each day together.

This day—
     when we chose each other,

This day—
     when we chose to grow in love

For years to come.

No one after lighting a lamp puts it under the bushel basket, but on the lamp stand, and it gives light to all in the house. In the same way, let your light shine before others, so that they may see your good works and give glory to your Father in heaven.

MATTHEW 5:15–16

A wedding is a witness that true love can be found.

I appeal to you therefore, brothers and sisters, by the mercies of God, to present your bodies as a living sacrifice, holy and acceptable to God, which is your spiritual worship.

ROMANS 12: 1–2

A wedding transforms a relationship from great to extraordinary.

Looking Back

There is a photograph that I often stop to admire.

We have rings on our fingers
and smiles on our faces.
It is Day One of our big adventure together.

What was most important to you on that day?
What do you remember most? What started it all?

Looking Ahead

Now we are husband and wife.
Some days are filled with joy,
other days are more difficult.

But our wedding photograph
tells the story of our dreams.

What is your dream for your marriage?
How can you keep your dreams alive?

Anniversary Prayer

God,

Today we celebrate our anniversary.
And we have grown together in love.

Help us make each year
a time to love and trust each other.

Give us the courage
to experience new things together
and discover you
as we love and honor
our commitment to each other.

Thank you for our love,
our struggles and joy
as we become a stronger,
wiser, and more loving couple.

With your love
in the year ahead.

Amen.

Attending Weddings

There we are
again

> The look in their eyes,
> the vows they share,
> the way they hold each other
> for their first dance.

There we are
again

> It's not
> the dress, the flowers, or the food

It's full of hope

Knowing only love
> is the most beautiful force on earth.

God,

We have chosen to build a life together.

Bless our marriage.

Help us to remember all that brought us to each other.

Help us to treasure each day together
    as we embrace all that is yet to be.

We are building a life together
through your love for us.

Bless our marriage,
we pray.

Amen.

Can you believe you are married? It might still seem like a dream. A wedding day isn't just something to be preserved in photos and memories. It is an ongoing invitation to grow in love and celebrate each day and each year. God has brought you together. Continue the celebration!

Sharing Together

✦ *What are your favorite memories of your wedding day?*

✦ *What are your favorite memories together since that day?*

✦ *How has your relationship grown the most since your wedding day?*

Growing Together

✦ *Pull out photographs, videos, guest books, or other items from your wedding day and relive your day together.*

✦ *Explore new possibilities together on your wedding anniversaries of one month, six months, or even a year. What is something you have always wanted to do as a couple?*

Chapter Five

LIVING AS ONE

Therefore a man leaves his father
and his mother and clings to his wife,
and they become one flesh.

GENESIS 2:24

Marriage is a
lifelong commitment to
grow in love together.

*M*y father and I woke up early the morning of my wedding day and headed to the restaurant of the hotel where all of my out-of-town relatives were staying. As my married friends and relatives arrived, my dad called them over to our table and said, "My son is getting married today. What advice do you have for him?" I heard all kinds of advice. Some were serious and some made me laugh. One of my cousins jokingly said, "Don't do it! Get out while you still can!"

Two bits of advice really made an impression on me that day. My uncle shared these words: "The more you put into your marriage, the more you will get out of it." My cousin said: "Marriage takes work. Every day you need to work to make your marriage better. If you do that, you can be very happy."

Since you first met, your relationship has grown and matured. Your feelings for each other have strengthened. Why? Because you have supported one another and grown in your feelings for one another.

When we are short on time, tired, or busy, it can be a little harder to give of ourselves or even receive, but that is part of getting to know one another.

My cousin said, "Marriage takes work." But what I think he meant is that marriage takes time and care, and being present to one another's need.

The best part is that you have the opportunity to grow closer together and become happier than you ever imagined.

What an amazing gift you have been given: a lifetime together! How do you want to spend that time?

One of my favorite sayings is,
"Love is a verb."

I've seen it in poems,
I've heard it in songs:
"Love is a verb."

What does it mean?

Some people may think
that love is a feeling.
And it is that, too!

The best part of love is that
as we love,
we feel love.

As we listen, support, care, and give of ourselves,
we feel love.

It's kind of a miracle
that goes round and round.

As time goes on,
we might fear that our feelings will fade.

What can we do?
Remember that love is a verb.

Loving God,

We want our love and trust to grow.
We want to love beyond any struggle.
We want to become better people
and a better couple.

We want to be good to one another
always.

Guide us in our commitment,
help us to understand one another
more and more.

Thank you for fun,
and love, and the joy of self-giving.

Help us trust in you
and each other
for a lifetime.

Amen.

The husband should give to his wife her conjugal rights, and likewise the wife to her husband.

1 CORINTHIANS 7:3

Marriage is a commitment to one another each day.

Each of you, however, should love his wife as himself, and a wife should respect her husband.

EPHESIANS 5:33

A happy marriage is two people placing each other's needs above their own.

Looking Back

Think about the time you have
spent together as a couple.

>   Fun
>   Challenging
>   Daily
>   Special
>   Loving times...

>   What have you loved most?

Looking Ahead

Your greatest gift is each other.
What would make you even happier?
How could your love grow stronger?
What would you love to do together the most?

Sometimes opposites attract.

A day at the park?
One wants to read or have a picnic.
The other wants to run or play soccer.

A day at the beach?
One wants to relax and *watch* the waves.
The other wants to adventurously *ride* the waves.

Sometimes opposites attract.

Take turns.
Learn something new.
Find activities you both enjoy.

Sometimes opposites attract.

Yet every day begins
with an amazing moment.

Waking up with love,
waking up with life lying next to you.

Sharing an amazing gift from God.

My cousin told me that marriage takes work, but what a great job! Putting each other's needs before our own, sharing common goals, discovering what we enjoy most, and being the best person we can be for each other. It's called daily love. It has become the foundation for our life together.

Sharing Together

✦ *What is your favorite way to spend time with your spouse?*

✦ *How have you grown in your love since your wedding day?*

✦ *What are you most grateful for having received in your marriage?*

Growing Together

✦ *Plan a fun, new way to spend time together. It may be something you have both wanted to do or a way to serve others.*

✦ *Take some time and dream together. Make a list of what you would like to have experienced in your marriage a year from now.*

Chapter Six

TWO FAMILIES BECOME ONE

As for me and my household,
we will serve the LORD.

JOSHUA 24:15

Forming a new
family means understanding
our values.

*I*n the days following my engagement to Sherry, we had the fun of sharing our announcement with family and friends. We received many good wishes, "Congratulations," "I'm so happy for you," "You make a great couple." What I remember most vividly were the first words spoken by two of Sherry's uncles after hearing our news. They each shook my hand and said, "Welcome to the family."

Marriage is not only about the joining of two families, it's the creation of a *new* family. Two people bring the experience of their own families and develop a relationship that will become a source of love, strength, and support for a lifetime.

The creation of a new family happens on the wedding day, but the uniqueness and stability form a little at a time, through ordinary and significant moments as a married couple.

Sometimes, forming a new family can be a little more difficult than we imagined. Families can love a couple very much, but their priorities and expectations can be far different from the couple's.

Families might also share different customs, ethnic backgrounds, or live thousands of miles from each other.

Sometimes you can combine the best of each family as you make decisions on how you will spend time together at holidays, on weekends, or on special occasions. You might even create your own path as you grow as a couple and create traditions that are distinctly your own.

"Welcome to the family" means something different to everyone, but the journey is yours to discover, shape, and experience as you begin your new life together. What will your new family be like?

When I was young,
  my father sometimes told me:

"When you marry a person, you marry a family."

I always thought the words made sense,
  but I didn't understand
  until I became engaged and married.

Two families becoming one:
  generous amounts of acceptance
  and understanding.

Two families becoming one:
  new values, attitudes, traditions.

My father was right,
  but the words need to change just a little:

"One of the best things about getting married
  is that you marry a family."

God,

We thank you for our parents,
grandparents,
siblings,
and extended family.

As we form our new family,
give us the wisdom
to create a life
centered on love,
happiness, and you.

As our marriage continues to grow,
help us support our family members
as they support us:

In a circle of life that gives life.

Amen.

Those who trouble their households will inherit wind,
  and the fool will be servant to the wise.

PROVERBS 11:29

Always strive to do what is best for your family.

And whoever does not provide for relatives, and especially
for family members, has denied the faith and is worse than
an unbeliever.

1 TIMOTHY 5:8

*Becoming a family means caring
for each other's as your own.*

Looking Back

Think about your family.
Now think of them on your wedding day.

Think about what you love most.
And what you remember most.
How do you see your family in you?

Looking Ahead

Think about the new family you are forming with your spouse.

What are your hopes?

Imagine the traits you might share, a holiday, time together.
What are your hopes?

Christmas Day is here
and now we must choose
traditions, food, gifts, family, days,
after a lifetime of celebration—one way.

What will our traditions be now?

Simple or elaborate?
Real tree or artificial?
Will we open presents on Christmas Eve
or Christmas Day?

And what kind of presents,
how many, for whom?

How will we make all of these small decisions
that are so big—as we make new memories together?

How will we celebrate together?

God bless our family,
new and beginning,
a heritage, and a lifetime.

Bless our words and actions
with one another
    to bring love and support.

Bless our future
    as we grow closer
    to each other.

God, bless our family and families.

May we grow together in you.

Amen.

"Welcome to the family" means new things each year, each holiday, each day, as two lives and two families become one.

As you create a new family, there is much to learn about each other and yourselves. As you grow together and celebrate together, your new family will continue to change, just as you do.

Joining our life with another is just the beginning of something bigger than we ever imagined; challenges, joy, open hearts, and a joined history through committed love. You are now a part of it all. Celebrate!

Sharing Together

✦ *What do you appreciate most about the families in which you grew up?*

✦ *What are the most valued traditions you each bring to your new family?*

✦ *What makes your new family unique, different from either of your families?*

Growing Together

✦ *Create a family tree of your new shared family. Share stories that will help you each get to know your new family.*

✦ *Start a new family tradition of your own. Use an existing holiday, or create a new one.*

Chapter Seven

INTIMACY AND ROMANCE

Let us go out early to the vineyards,
and *see* whether the vines have budded,
whether the grape blossoms have opened
and the pomegranates are in bloom.
There I will give you my love.

SONG OF SONGS 7:12

Intimacy is most fulfilling
in a life-giving, committed
relationship of love.

*I*ntimacy and romance help tell the story of every relationship. When you remember the earliest days of your dating relationship, you may remember the exact date and the details of the first time you held hands, your first kiss, and your first date. In marriage, we express our love to one another intimately and romantically in many ways. Of course, physical intimacy quickly comes to mind as a personal and beautiful expression of love, but it is certainly not the only way to share love.

It can be a little awkward to think about and then talk about what expressions of intimacy are most meaningful, but it can also be a wonderful discovery.

In his book *The Five Love Languages: How to Express Heartfelt Commitment to Your Mate*, Gary Chapman identifies five ways, among the many ways, that couples express and receive love. They are: quality time, words of affirmation, gifts, acts of service, and physical touch.

While a spouse might not have ever thought about it, he or she might value quality time and physical touch, whereas the other might find that words of affirmation and acts of service touch him or her.

Of course, everyone is different. That's one reason it can be helpful to talk about each person's needs, even though it is not always an easy conversation. However, understanding one another better on any level can lead to better relating and a more fulfilling marriage.

Romance is sometimes defined as "a feeling of excitement and mystery associated with love." When you and your spouse first started dating, it probably didn't take much to make your new relationship seem exciting or mysterious. After all, everything you did together was new. Now that you are married, romance can seem elusive when everyday routines may not seem exciting or mysterious.

But that doesn't mean they aren't! I hope you are growing as a person each day, so it should come as no surprise that your spouse is, too. That is the beauty of growing in relationship. That is the intimacy of marriage.

We have so much love to share.
Whether we travel many miles
or stay in one place,

We share a journey
of commitment and love.

Our eyes meet and
our hearts beat together.

Joined by passion and devotion,
we touch
hearts, hands, minds, souls,
instinctive to one another's needs.

Each day, each night
I feel lucky and in love.

We have so much love to share.
Our journey to each other's hearts
will continue.

God, we thank you

>for your unconditional love,
>the closeness that we share
>learning day by day.

Help us love each other more fully,
more completely,
more selflessly.

Inspire us to express our love
daily, always,
moment by moment,
intimate and passionate;
words and actions
>protected and cherished.

Help us to continue to learn about each other.

As our love for each other continues to grow,
unending, always, forever.

Amen.

Pleasant words are like a honeycomb,
  sweetness to the soul and health to the body.

PROVERBS 16:24

Caring and considerate words build intimacy.

Let him kiss me with the kisses of his mouth!
For your love is better than wine.

SONG OF SONGS 1:2

Unconditional, committed,
marital love is powerful,
personal, intimate...enduring.

Looking Back

Think back to the early days of your relationship.

What were your favorite intimate moments?

What was it like:
  the day you met?
  the first time you held hands?
  the first time you shared something personal?

Looking Ahead

Imagine a perfect night of intimacy and romance.

What is important?
What shouldn't be missed?
What would be a wonderful surprise?

We were newlyweds,
>	a new city, new home, new jobs.

"Do you want to try taking dance lessons?"
>	my wife asked me one day.

>>	"Really?"
>>	"Please?"
>>	"OK, I'll do it for you."

I wouldn't describe our dancing as graceful,
>	but we laughed a lot
>	and learned a little
>>		about anticipation....

For that one hour, nothing else mattered in our lives.

We looked into each other's eyes
>	and learned how to
>	anticipate each other's moves,
>	and get a little more in sync.

It turns out I love to dance.

Or maybe it was just that one hour to hold each other
>	and have nothing else matter in our lives.

God,

Bless the time
we spend together as a couple.

Bless the words we speak.

Bless the gifts we share.

Bless the service we offer.

Bless our intimate moments.

Bless all our expressions of love,

You, the giver of all love.

Amen.

Enjoying committed marital intimacy each day is one of the greatest blessings of marriage. Whether you have been married one year or fifty years, you can still enjoy romantic, intimate moments together.

Remember, intimacy is different for everyone. A wedding day is the beginning of a lifetime to explore the many ways to support one another in good times and bad and all the times in between.

Sharing Together

✦ *What is your favorite way of showing love to your spouse?*

✦ *What have you learned about romance and intimacy since your wedding day?*

✦ *What do you enjoy most about intimacy or romance?*

Growing Together

✦ *Ask your spouse, "What is your idea of an evening of romance?" Then listen to each other and start planning.*

✦ *Keep a list of new things you and your spouse would like to do together. Keep it by a calendar and make each item on the list a reality, one month at a time.*

Chapter Eight

FIGHTING AND DISILLUSIONMENT

Love is patient; love is kind; love is not envious or boastful or arrogant or rude. It does not insist on its own way; it is not irritable or resentful; it does not rejoice in wrongdoing, but rejoices in the truth. It bears all things, believes all things, hopes all things, endures all things.

1 CORINTHIANS 13:4–7

Love for each other will help you beyond all else.

*I*t may have happened just hours after your wedding. It might have taken a few days, or maybe even several weeks or months—but there is always a first fight in any relationship and in any marriage. Words of anger or frustration are exchanged, and you realize that as wonderful as the wedding was, the real world is here to greet you.

Every couple is unique, as is every marriage. Likewise, every couple has come from a marriage with various ways of handling conflict, so patterns of doing so will be different for each spouse. Yet it can be devastating when any couple finds themselves fighting or in a disagreement, especially shortly after beginning a marriage.

My parents are the most compatible married couple I have ever known. They have a lot in common, they are extremely considerate of one another, and they never seem to disagree about anything. In fact, I have never heard them raise their voices to one another.

For me, they were an incredible example of what I thought all happy marriages were supposed to be, with no disagreements of any kind. You can imagine what a shock it was for to me to quarrel with my spouse after getting married.

At first, I thought I was failing as a husband. Then I realized that a successful marriage and any relationship is founded more on how you treat each other during conflicts, rather than whether or not you disagree about anything.

You will probably spend more time with your spouse

than any other person for the rest of your life. So it is likely that you will differ at some point about something.

However, if you are committed to care, love, and respect—even when tempers flare—you will form bonds in your marriage that become bridges to understanding, rather than chasms of miscommunication or escalating arguments.

We are fighting again.
Hurtful words have been exchanged,
feelings have been hurt.

We are ashamed, knowing that our marriage
        has turned into this.

God,
help us to listen to one another
and to hear.

Guide us
to patience, understanding,
and support for one another.

We have faith that, through you,
our home will once again be a place
        where your love will reign.

Show us the first step
        and then each one after that
        back to you
        and back to each other.

We know how wonderful our marriage can be,
And we have faith that we can return to that place.

God,
Help us to love and respect each other,
        to share true, unconditional love
        that will grow as we grow in our marriage.

We envisioned a lifetime of happiness.

Now we share
        a messy and unorganized home,
        disappointment in one another,
        fatigue, disillusionment

…and sometimes, hurtful words and actions.

We fear we have failed
at marriage, at love.

God, help us understand
        that you are there,
        as is our love,
        right on the other side of this argument,
        right beyond the fear.

Strengthen our marriage
        and help us find each other again.

Amen.

Why do you see the speck in your neighbor's eye, but do not notice the log in your own eye? Or how can you say to your neighbor, "Let me take the speck out of your eye", while the log is in your own eye? You hypocrite, first take the log out of your own eye, and then you will see clearly to take the speck out of your neighbor's eye.

MATTHEW 7:3–5

Look with the eye of the other. Then solve it together.

[Jesus said,] "If you forgive the sins of any, they are forgiven them; if you retain the sins of any, they are retained."

JOHN 20:23

Spouses who forgive
are able to move forward.
Spouses who hold grudges
can create barriers.

Looking Back

Think about a disagreement
    between you and your love,
    days or years ago,
    that you now feel terrible about
    what you said or how you acted.
What would you do differently?
What did you learn about yourself?
What can you do now?

Looking Ahead

Think about the future of your marriage.
How can believe and trust each other best?
The days you experience now will help you get there.
What can you do now?

Everybody has a breaking point,

When my wife reaches her limit, she explodes.
Then she can think clearly.

When I reach my limit, I say nothing
and try to work it out inside.

Is one better than the other? Does it matter?

What matters is that we know how
　　　to support each other.

We're not perfect, but we can recover
　　　from difficult times,
　　　as long as we know we are still there
　　　for each other.

That's what marriage is all about.

God,

Bless our eyes
    as we look at each other with respect.

Bless our ears
    as we listen attentively to one another.

Bless our mouths
    as we speak considerate words.

Bless our hands
    as we show love and concern.

Bless our hearts
    as we care for each other with passion.

Bless our marriage,
    our love for each other,
    our love for you.

Amen.

Disagreements occur in any relationship. When they happen, we can show love and respect as we search for common ground. The reward for doing this is enormous. Love and respect can lead to a better understanding of each other, fuller trust, and stronger love.

Sharing Together

✦ *What are the sensitive issues that lead to conflict? What is at the heart? What is in your heart?*

✦ *What will help you support one another more completely when you disagree?*

✦ *What would make fighting easier for you?*

Growing Together

✦ *Create a strategy for what to do when struggles arise. What steps can you take as a couple to ensure your values will hold, despite your disagreement? Write down each step and ask God's blessing on your plan.*

✦ *Set up a regular time to talk about what could go better; maybe once a month. Listen to each other without judging or jumping in to solve a problem. Then talk about how you can support each other.*

Chapter Nine

ENCOUNTERING CHANGE

For everything there is a season, and a time for
every matter under heaven:
a time to be born, and a time to die;
a time to plant, and a time to pluck up
      what is planted;
a time to kill, and a time to heal;
a time to break down, and a time to build up;
a time to weep, and a time to laugh;
a time to mourn, and a time to dance.

ECCLESIASTES 3:1–4

Life is full of change.

The only thing that never changes is change. We can plan for some changes, anticipate others, but some still come as a complete surprise—and will keep coming. To live is to change.

Occasionally, I've heard people say, "I don't deal well with change." Yet life is an ongoing series of changes. Some are small, some are bigger, and marriage brings some of the most significant changes of all.

Newly married couples have a massive amount of change to adjust to in a short amount of time. Moving to a new home, expanding social circles, financial decisions, shared schedules, and including another in all your decisions amount to quite a bit of change!

Then—just to complicate it all—we are changing inside. Somehow we forget that our opinions, accomplishments, goals, and priorities will continue to change even amid all the newness we are encountering as newlyweds.

Your relationship as a couple will also continue to evolve as you learn more about each other and experience the many changes that come with beginning a new life together.

As a married couple, and as individuals, we always have an important choice to make when we encounter change. We can fight it every time it comes into our life, or we can accept it, adapt to it, and realize it is ever-present in our relationship and our lives.

You might even learn to enjoy this unfolding adventure, especially since resistance can bring perpetual frustration.

The other important choice that is always present when change occurs is how to support your spouse during times of change or how to take care of yourself if you are having an experience that involves change.

We may not like it, but change—like our need to breathe—does not go away.

The temperature rising outside

Wildflowers blooming in a field

Kittens playing on the lawn

A freshly painted room

A newly ripened peach

A weather broadcast predicting hail

A newborn child

To live is to change.

Change is life.

God, we both wanted to be married,
but we didn't want to change.

Now we are married,
and the changes seem to come all the time.

We prepared for some of the changes,
    but others have surprised us,
    or are more difficult than we imagined.

God, help us not to fear these changes.

Help us to embrace changes together.

Help us to become stronger, closer,
and better able to support one another.

Help us remember
our unchanging love
for you,
for each other.

That we can change

    Despite all our doubt.

Amen.

Every generous act of giving, with every perfect gift, is from above, coming down from the Father of lights, with whom there is no variation or shadow due to change.

JAMES 1:17

God's unconditional love for us never changes.

So if anyone is in Christ, there is a new creation: everything old has passed away; see, everything has become new!

2 CORINTHIANS 5:17

Placing Christ in the center of your marriage is a good change!

Looking Back

Think back to
>   the day you met each other,
>   your wedding day,
>   today.

How have you changed?
How has your spouse changed?
How have your priorities changed?

Looking Ahead

Imagine your life together
>   next year, or the year after.

What do you hope for most?

What do you hope will never change?
What would be a good change?

Five to ten years from now,
what do you hope will never change?

Indiana or California?

We both wanted to be near our families.

We planned a wedding and a move at the same time.

New jobs, a new home, a new life together.

Then—an incredible job offer!
And we moved cross-country again.

So much change!
Learning together,
making decisions,
forming a life,
changing together.

We wouldn't change a thing.

Constant God,

When anticipation fills us with excitement,

When anticipation fills us with fear,

When the unexpected leads us to happiness,

When the unexpected knocks us to the ground,

When we do not fully understand your plan for us,

When we try to follow your plan,

Be with us!

In good times and in bad,
for richer or poorer, in sickness, and in health.

To live is to change.

Amen.

Change is inevitable, but you have three incredible gifts that will help you encounter change.

First, you have God's unconditional love, which will never disappear or fade.

Second, you have a life partner with whom you can face any challenge, hand-in-hand.

Third, your strong, ever-evolving marriage can help support you as you navigate life's many changes.

Sharing Together

+ *What difficult change have you survived well?*

+ *What qualities as a couple help you deal with change?*

+ *What potential changes scare you the most?*
  What can you do now to alleviate your fear?

Growing Together

+ *Look at photographs or mementos from throughout your relationship. What has changed?*

+ *Decide one change that you would like to make as a couple. What needs to change to make it happen?*

Chapter Ten

SOLVING PROBLEMS TOGETHER

[Jesus said,] "Therefore I tell you, do not worry about your life, what you will eat or what you will drink, or about your body, what you will wear. Is not life more than food, and the body more than clothing? Look at the birds of the air; they neither sow nor reap nor gather into barns, and yet your heavenly Father feeds them. Are you not of more value than they? And can any of you by worrying add a single hour to your span of life?"

MATTHEW 6:25–27

Trust that God is
watching over you.

"*A*nd they lived happily ever after..."

When I read bedtime stories to my children, I notice that many classic fairy tales end with this line. The entire story may focus on how two people fell in love, but all we hear about the rest of their lives together is "they lived happily ever after."

While I believe marriage can lead to a lifetime of happiness, life can still present us with challenges, whether we are single or married. However, married couples have the advantage and challenge of facing difficulties together, rather than individually.

So what problems will you face as a couple? Ironically, the biggest problem may be thinking there won't be any problems. You are both human, after all! And you live in an all-too-human world.

So, even if your relationship is free from struggle, outside events can bring unexpected stress or concern. However, your support for each other can carry you through the changes in your own relationship and any problems you encounter.

Even though married couples know one another intimately, it is likely that you and your spouse will learn more about each other as you grow and live together, especially when you encounter problems in your relationship.

Whether problems come from outside or inside a relationship, the key to solving them together is to be open with one another.

Without communicating well, even tiny problems can

evolve into huge difficulties. However, if couples can express feelings and ideas with one another and really listen to each other, a foundation and pattern can be built for how you will solve problems whenever they arise.

Surprisingly, solving problems together can actually strengthen your relationship, as well as your love for each other, and better prepare you for any future problems that come your way.

Everyone wants to be right.

Turn on the TV or listen to the radio
and you'll hear "experts" fiercely debating
     how they are right—about everything.

This may work in television and radio studios,
     but it doesn't work so well in marriage.

If you spend your time arguing about who's right,
     one person will be right,
     and one person won't.

Is it worth it?

In division there is no right or wrong,
there is only division.

Life sometimes seems so overwhelming.

We just want to be happy.

We work so hard to solve our problems,
　　and then new ones pop up to take their place.

God, help us to see problems
　　as invitations
　　to accomplish something amazing

　　together.

For there is hope for a tree,
   if it is cut down, that it will sprout again,
   and that its shoots will not cease.
Though its root grows old in the earth,
   and its stump dies in the ground,
yet at the scent of water it will bud
   and put forth branches like a young plant.

JOB 14:7–9

Never lose hope!

I can do all things through him who strengthens me.

PHILIPPIANS 4:13

Through God, all things are possible.

Looking Back

Think about small problems you experienced
  before your marriage.

Which problems were easily solved?
Which problems turned into big problems?

Did you solve problems alone or reach out for help?

Looking Ahead

Think about small problems you have experienced
  since your marriage.

Which problems were easily solved?
Have any problems turned into bigger problems?

Did you solve problems alone or reach out for help?

We needed a new car, but we had little to spend.
My wife had only one request.

"Please, don't buy a stick shift," she pleaded.
"I've never driven one."

My father and I shopped all day,
and we finally found it—the car!

It was wonderful and deeply discounted.
There was only one left, and we had to act fast.
Oh no! It's a stick shift!

She had only made one request, but I ignored it.

After the tears dried and the anger faded,
at least a little,

We spent every night in an empty parking lot
learning how to drive the car.

We learned a lot together through that car.

I have never bought another stick shift.

God,

Bless our minds,
as we think about how
to solve problems together.

Bless our conversations,
as we share our thoughts and feelings
attentively, respectfully.

Bless our hearts,
as we solve this problem.

With your faith in us
and our faith in each other.

Amen.

Marriage offers incredible gifts—support, perspective, and commitment to be together when problems arise. Your individual strengths and care for each other can help you learn to solve problems together and create a wonderful life with one another.

As your ability to trust in one another and in God continues to grow, any problem can become an opportunity to thrive in love and faith.

Sharing Together

✦ *What helps you solve problems together as a couple?*

✦ *What strengths do you each bring to solving problems?*

✦ *How can your strength support your spouse?*

Growing Together

✦ *Buy a jigsaw puzzle with lots of pieces and work on it together. Talk about how you each approach puzzle solving.*

✦ *Make a list of problems you currently experience or that you might face in the near future. What can you do to help each other?*

Chapter Eleven

GOD IN OUR MARRIAGE

All who have sinned apart from the law
will also perish apart from the law,
and all who have sinned under the law
will be judged by the law.

ROMANS 2:12

Centering your lives
on God offers a
new level of happiness
and fulfillment.

*W*hat did you wish for when you used to dream about marriage, even before you met "the one?" Did you hope to have an ordinary marriage, or one that would be truly spectacular, with amazing love and closeness with your spouse?

Perhaps the best marriages include both—one where the ordinary is truly spectacular. As with most things, the choices we make every day help determine happiness. However, one choice can make all the difference in a marriage. That's the choice to make God the center your marriage.

It's easy to get so caught up in "stuff" that we push God aside. "We don't have time." This might be an attitude that creeps into our marriage as well. "We don't have time" to listen, to enjoy time together, to grow in our relationship.

In the same way that our relationship with our spouse can diminish if we don't take time to connect, so it is with God.

As newlyweds, my wife and I didn't make the effort to include God in our daily lives. We fell into stressful routines of busyness and lost our closeness with one another. Worst of all, our lives seemed to have lost meaning. We were busy, but what was the point? What were we really trying to achieve?

We decided to find a church community where we felt welcome and where we could get involved. We also started praying on a regular basis, individually and as a couple.

We discovered that serving others also helped us grow in our faith, so we looked for opportunities to serve as a couple.

In the end, we found a renewed connection with one another as we renewed our relationship with God. Although we were already in love, we came to be even more committed.

All married couples want to feel loved. God is the inventor of love. We found ourselves again by coming back to the source of our love.

It's a miracle!

God created the miracle of marriage
    so we might realize and cherish

God's love for each other
    even more....

The ultimate love story.

God of all marriages,
You are the source of the love
we have for each other.

Help us remember
    that by taking time to say thank you,
    by sharing our needs with you,
    by trusting your guidance,
    our marriage will become even better.

Help us remember
    that by taking time to thank each other,
    by sharing our needs with each other,
    by trusting each other,
    our marriage will become even better.

Help us to make you the center of our lives.

You, the source of our love.

Amen.

God is our refuge and strength,
  a very present help in trouble.
  Therefore we will not fear,
      though the earth should change,
  though the mountains shake in the heart of the sea;
  though its waters roar and foam,
  though the mountains tremble with its tumult.

PSALM 46:1–3

*Placing God in the center provides strength,
even during difficult times.*

Trust in the LORD with all your heart,
  and do not rely on your own insight.

PROVERBS 3:5

*In good times and difficult times,
trust in God.*

Looking Back

Think about how your relationship with God
    has changed since you were young,
    since you have married.

How did you imagine God?
How did you communicate with God?

    How did you want to communicate with God?
    How has God led you to your spouse?

Looking Ahead

How would you like to see God present in your marriage?
How would you like your spouse to see God's love through
you?

I imagined that one day, if I was lucky,
    I would marry a wonderful woman,
    and she would love God.

Years passed, and we met and married.
Now we love God together.

Serving others has brought us closer together
    and given our marriage a greater purpose.

Our love for each other
    has helped make the world better.

    In God, the source of love.

God,

Thank you for bringing us
     together.

For our love is only possible
     because of your love for us.

Bless our marriage
with your love and guidance,

so we can continue
to serve those around us
and love one another.

Amen.

Do you want your marriage to be ordinary or extraordinary? In God's eyes, our marriage is never less than extraordinary. God's never-ending love for us makes all things extraordinary! It's never too late to invite God's presence into your marriage.

Love is the mystery that brought you and your spouse together. May that same mystery continue to draw you deeper and deeper in love and faith.

Sharing Together

✦ *Share what your relationship with God is like right now.*

✦ *What do you do as a couple to center your marriage on God? What would you like to do?*

✦ *How could you serve those around you as a married couple?*

Growing Together

✦ *Pray together as a couple. Thank God for all you love about your spouse. Be specific. Perhaps write it down and then take turns each day naming one thing from your list as you pray together.*

✦ *Identify someone who might be able to use your help. Offer your help as a couple and let God use your love for each other to help others.*

Chapter Twelve

DREAMS
AHEAD

For surely I know the plans I have for you,
says the LORD, plans for your welfare
and not for harm, to give you a future
with hope.

JEREMIAH 29:11

God has an incredible
vision of what your
marriage can become.

*F*or much of your life, your dream might have been about "the one." You probably wondered, "Who will this person be? What will this person be like? How will this person make me happy?"

Not only have these questions been answered, but at your wedding you promised each other a lifetime together. Dreams do come true!

Your dreams as a married couple are like fingerprints. No two are exactly alike, and they help define who you are as a couple. As you live your married life around God and as you grow in love together, you can begin to dream together.

One of our earliest dreams as a couple was to go white-water rafting together. During our engagement, we planned a rafting trip, rode the rapids, and shared an unforgettable experience together.

When we married, we continued to think about what we wanted and dreamed about as a couple. Sherry and I both wanted to have a family, and we now have three children. Day by day, we are fulfilling our dreams of a family and creating new dreams as our children grow.

Just as we once guided our little raft down a powerful and unpredictable river, our dreams are helping us navigate through life to find real and lasting happiness, with God as our center.

As a child, I was told God had a plan for me.

I thought, "That's not fair! I want my own plan!"

But what would it be like
if I already knew God's plan for me?

When I encountered people or possibilities,
would I just walk away from them?

Would I miss chances for discovery and growth?

Would I miss all the anticipation and searching
to find "the one?"

I would live without wonder.

I would never learn how to trust you, God,
with my life,
with the life of my spouse.

I would never have to discover my dreams.

Somehow, I'm glad I don't know God's plan.

God, I'm ready to discover my dreams on your time.

God, help us remember
    that you have a plan for us.

Help us place love
    in the center
    of everything we do.

Not just our love for each other,
    but your love for us.

Help us create and discover our dreams,
    your dream for us.

Dreams that bring a lifetime of happiness.

Dreams that bring forth love, and life, and more life.

God, help us remember
    that you have a plan for us.

Help us place love
    in the center
    of everything we do.

Amen.

Let love be genuine; hate what is evil, hold fast to what is good; love one another with mutual affection; outdo one another in showing honor.

ROMANS 12:9–10

Make love the treasure of your marriage.

Though your beginning was small,
your latter days will be very great.

JOB 8:7

As you grow together in love,
your marriage will bring you even greater
happiness and fulfillment.

Looking Back

What was your earliest childhood dream?

What was your dream for your life?

What did you dream about for your marriage?

Looking Ahead

What is your greatest dream for your marriage?

What is your greatest dream for your spouse?

What do you hope for most from God?

I just returned home
  from my best friend's wedding.

I witnessed a miracle.

Two people, born thousands of miles apart,
  discovered their love
  was their treasure.

They found each other,
  and now their hearts are full of new dreams.

They realized
  that, hand-in-hand,
  all things are possible,
  and that dreams can come true.

I witnessed a miracle.
  I am living a miracle
  with my true love.

God of miracles and love,

May we live each day as a married couple
    with a spirit of hope.

May we create dreams together

And pursue them
    passionately,
    with our entire heart, soul, and mind.

May we remember that as we change,
    our dreams may change,
    but you never change.

May we never forget that,
    through your love
    and our love for each other,
    all things are possible.

Bless our future together,

God of miracles and love.

Amen.

Dreams help define the person we are, and the person we will become. As you continue to love each other and embrace the dreams that grow out of your love, look to God to help you as you make them come true together.

Sharing Together

✦ *How did your dreams change when you met your spouse?*

✦ *What is your greatest dream as a couple?*

✦ *What is your greatest dream for your love together?*

Growing Together

✦ *Write a letter to your spouse about your love and dreams for him or her in your marriage. Read each other's letters aloud to one another, then store them to read again, perhaps a year later.*

✦ *List five dreams you would like to come true as a couple. Decide how to make one happen—then the next one!*

"Love is to will the good of another."

SAINT THOMAS AQUINAS

ARCADIA PUBLIC LIBRARY
ARCADIA, WI 54612